DIARY OF
A MYSTICAL DRAGONFLY

by Barbara Ann Simone

Illustrated by Sarah Pecorino

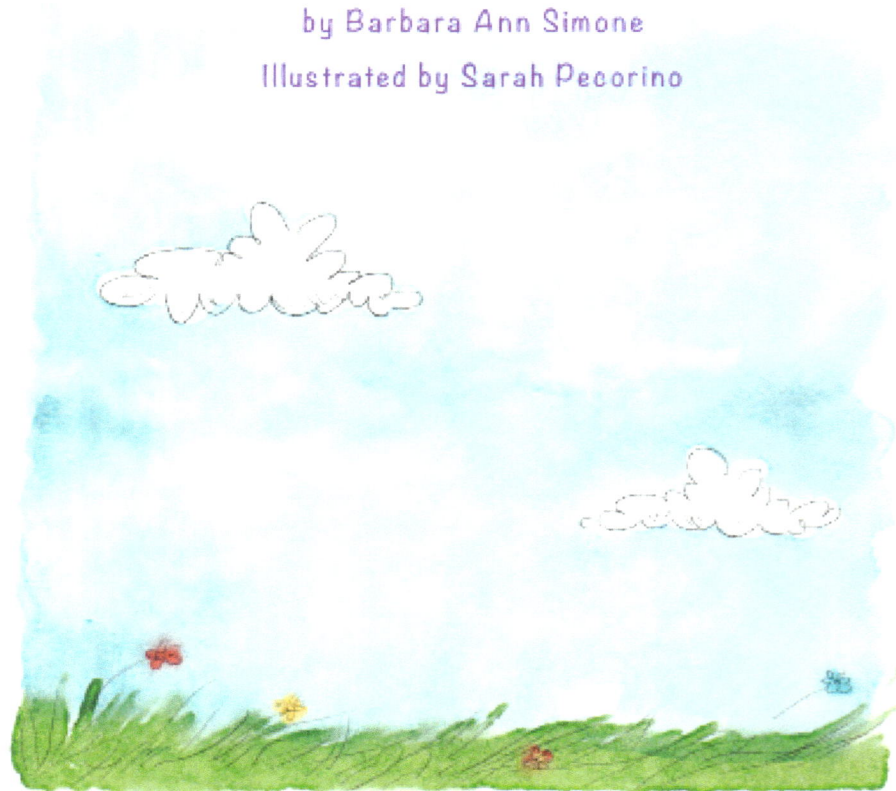

KIDS' GRIEF RELIEF

Hi, I'm Mystie.
What's
Dragon - You - Down ?

www.KidsGriefRelief.org

A 501(c)(3) NonProfit

Grief Support to Empower Bereaved Children

Copyright © 2014 Kids' Grief Relief

ISBN: 978-0-9856334-0-0

(softcover book)

DIARY OF A MYSTICAL DRAGONFLY !

a.k.a. FOR THE LOVE OF DARVY

CONTENTS

I AM A MYSTICAL DRAGONFLY

Do you believe in life on other planets? Because if you don't, you probably won't believe what I'm about to tell you. I hope you keep on reading, because I bet by the end of this story, you WILL BELIEVE!

My name is Mystie. My full name is Mystic A. Dragonfly. Friends and family call me Mystie. Even though I prefer to be called Mystie, there are moments when I REALLY like being referred to as Mystic.

A Mystic is someone who is very aware of the connection to his or her own powerful, inner spirit. I'd like to think that's who I am, or who I always try to be. When I feel connected to that inner part of me, I feel my best.

Do you know that feeling?

I'm not talking about the inside stuff like your bones and muscles. I'm talking about the part of you that's MORE than that. It's called "spirit"; something you can't really see, but you can feel. It's the part of you that knows what's best for you, at all times.

Take a deep breath right now and relax. Good. Now think of something or someone you love. Got it? Doesn't that feel good inside? You connected with YOUR inner spirit.

The dragonflies of my home planet, Nilrem, are all mystical in nature. So Mystic A. Dragonfly is a very good name for me. But please call me Mystie, because I love having lots of friends.

Nilrem is filled with magical dragonflies. Does that sound strange? I won't tell you too much about Nilrem right now, except that it's a really neat place to live. It's quite different from your planet Earth, even though your planet is as beautiful as Nilrem. We have unique, beautifully colored plants and flowers like Earth, but our soil is a blue-violet color that reflects light.

The biggest difference between Earth and Nilrem is in the way everybody thinks, feels, and lives. On planet Nilrem, all things live in peace and harmony. There has never been war. We understand and honor how we're all connected by Love.

I think more and more Earthlings are starting to get this idea. Things are changing. There's lots of GOOD happening on Earth right now.

By the way, I am not only Mystical; I am also quite Magical!

The kind of magic you have on Earth is fun and weird at the same time. I like watching your magic tricks because it's hard to figure out how some of your magicians do what they do. The tricks are very impressive and entertaining.

Of course I think the kind of Magic I use is the **most** impressive, because it comes from within me.

It took me a long time to learn this (and you may not want to hear it) but there's one idea that's exactly the same for Nilremian dragonflies as it is for you wonderful humans.

"PRACTICE MAKES PERFECT."

How many times have you heard *that?*
Now you're hearing it from me. Practice makes perfect.

I needed perfect Magic to save me, when I first came to your planet. I wasn't ready for the shocking thing that happened, but I'm getting ahead of myself.

The best way for me to tell you my story is to first explain how I learned Magic. It started with my magnificent wings. Do you see the hearts and stars on them? I actually created them with my own inner power. Now THAT'S MAGICAL!

CHAPTER TWO

I GROW MY WINGS

Like all Nilremian dragonflies, when I was hatched from the water, I didn't have any wings. I looked like a small walking bug, moving around on my six legs. There were eleven of us dragonflies that hatched at the same time, and we were all walking around. Actually, I can't really call us dragon-*flies*. A better name for us would be dragon-walkers. So we dragon-walkers became a team and decided to work together to learn how to use Magic.

No Magic = No Flying.

That was the ONE thing we all understood.

The elder dragonflies, mostly our parents and other relatives, would give us hints each week. We had to figure out what the hints meant, and try them out for ourselves.

Our families knew it was best for us to learn how to use our inner powers by ourselves, rather than for them to tell us exactly what to do. It worked, but it took some time.

By the way, Nilremians **Love** to talk in rhyme. I'll try to remember that you might not like rhymes, except I haven't found one song that Earthlings listen to that **doesn't** rhyme! So if you'd like to, go ahead and sing any music you like underneath all of the magical hints and messages from Nilrem.

This was the most important hint:

The Magic of your wings is this
They grow from what's inside.
> *Your thoughts and feelings are the key,*
> *So expand your Love to fly!*
>> *Focus, little dragonflies*
>> *Expand your Love to fly,*
>>> *Focus, little dragonflies*
>>> *Expand your Love to fly!*

I understood some of what they said. I was born with the wisdom of Nilrem inside of me. Earth children are born pretty smart too. Seems to me they have lots of new, creative ideas to offer adults.

Anyway, there I was with my other dragon-walk friends, thinking about what we all just heard. We really wanted to start flying, so we thought and thought and thought some more. We went inside our hearts, trying to feel the answer. And guess what? After all my dragon-walker friends and I did all that thinking and feeling, we all got the same answer.

LOVE

We all said "no way!" because at first it seemed too simple. Everyone, even Earthlings, understand the power of Love.

Every Nilremian, even the tiniest one, knows that Love energy created Nilrem and all the living things that walk and crawl and fly in and around it. We knew we had Love inside us, but we still didn't have our wings. What did we not understand?

So we thought and thought some more. Inside me, I kept seeing the word "focus," and my good friend, Merly, kept hearing the word "expand", inside of him.

So we focused AND expanded the Love we felt for ourselves and all of Nilrem.
And guess what?

Our wings started to grow! Being mystical helped me be magical!

We performed our Magic every day. The more we focused deeply on love, stars started appearing and forming our wings; the more we FELT love deeply, the more hearts added to the formation of our wings. When we spoke our feelings and thoughts out loud, the hearts and stars grew bolder and bolder in color, until they actually glowed. Shazaam!

That was how our inner powers worked. We created our awesome wings. So "practice DID make perfect".

I also found out that in order to *keep flying*, I had to stay focused on LOVE. That was a hard lesson. I can't tell you how many times I crashed into a tree because I stopped focusing. It wasn't that I was having thoughts that weren't loving, it was just that I wasn't thinking or feeling much of anything, kind of daydreaming, I guess. Then, CRASH! OUCH! My wings would freeze up, and I would nose-dive into a bunch of branches or thorns. I probably crashed ten or even fifteen times before I really learned how to fly the way I wanted to, and do it all the time.

For a while I heard a lot of CRASHes and OUCHes all over the forest. My friends were learning the same lesson. We all learned that lesson the "long" way.

So as we mastered our inner powers, we were soon flying and soaring all over Nilrem. Proudly, we knew we had finally become Dragon-flies!

We celebrated our Magical accomplishment for days and days. As we flew, we sang and danced, making large circles in the sky. We got silly and played thrill-seeking games. That's one of the best memories I have of Nilrem.

CHAPTER THREE

I FLY TO EARTH

My family and I traveled around Nilrem a lot, discovering new sights together. I wanted to explore more than anything else in the Universe!

One day, my grandfather told me about other planets I could visit. Some of them sounded quite interesting, but not interesting enough for me to tour. Then he told me about planet Earth. He said there were dragonflies there. He said they weren't like us, but they WERE called *dragonflies* just the same. That really caught my attention!

Later, when I announced that I was going to fly to Earth to meet one, I was totally shocked at how my family reacted. They all said,

"THAT'S NOT THE BEST PLACE FOR YOU!"

When I asked why not, they told me it might be very hard to use my Magic there.

That sounded ridiculous. After all, I AM a Mystical, Magical Dragonfly, who has mastered the use of my inner powers to create wings and fly. I told them I was a great Magician who had learned the lessons of flight very well on Nilrem. That was that.

They agreed that I knew how to use Magic, yet one or two of my relatives looked like they wanted to say something else. Before they spoke, Grandpa took me aside to speak to me privately; he usually does that when he feels strongly about something. I listened intently as he told me it had been a long time since a Nilremian dragonfly had visited Earth, and when one had come back, he'd told stories that were shocking and unsettling to Nilremians. When I demanded to know what in the Universe he was talking about, he became silent. That's unusual for Grandpa, who always knows what to say.

Finally, after what seemed hours, all he would say was that I would see things on Earth that could be difficult for me. IF I decided to go, I had to remember how to use my Magic anytime I got into trouble. That was dumb. Like I was going to forget what I learned. I thanked Grandpa and flew away. I got the feeling he was trying to protect me from something, but what could that be?

So now Earth became even *more* interesting. As days and weeks went by, I couldn't get Earth out of my head. I was intrigued.

I had to find out what made Earth such a secretive place, and why Grandpa was trying to protect me. It was an adventure I couldn't resist. So very determined, I went back to Grandpa.

I told him I REALLY wanted to explore Earth and meet some dragonflies.

"I've decided, Grandpa. I'm going to Earth."

Grandpa's violet-colored magic hat seemed to be alive, its blue stars glowing against the Nilremian night sky. He looked at me as if he were sizing me up for a job. He nodded his head once and said,

"Mystie, you're old enough and smart enough to fly wherever you want to fly. You've heard my advice about what you need to do when you're there. The rest is up to you."

"I know I'm responsible for my decisions, Grandpa," I replied. "Don't worry, I'm up to the challenge. I'll be back soon enough to let you know all about what I learn."

I spent the rest of the week telling my friends about my decision. They were excited to think about the time when I would come home again with all my Earth stories. My friend, Merly, said he would really miss me, and I told him I would miss him, too. I loved his green magic hat and the green, yellow and orange wings he created with his magic. We had spent lots of time exploring Nilrem and making new friends.

My family gave me a celebration that felt way too serious, but I still enjoyed myself because I felt very grown up. I had made a decision and I was going to stick with it. Good for me. I imagined myself flying home soon enough to tell them all how silly they were to think I couldn't use my Magic on some other planet.

Then off I went. Flying faster than the speed of light, which is impossible for Earthlings at this time, I flew toward Earth. I was wise enough to fly by thinking loving thoughts for myself and for Earth, and feeling Love for this new planet I was about to discover.

My Magic was the power that got me to Earth and that would get me back faster than the speed of light whenever I wanted to come home. I believed that would never change.

As I drew closer to Earth, I was delighted to see how much of your planet is covered in water. I chose to settle near an ocean, in a marshy beach full of white sand and tall grasses. I met pelicans, seagulls, sandpipers, and osprey.

One thing that was really neat about all the birds and animals I met was that they never judged me because I was different. When I told them I was from another planet, they didn't seem to flinch. They had no issues about me looking different either. I actually think they all liked the idea that I was from another planet.

My first close friend, Lark the bottlenose dolphin, was a wonderful guide who helped me settle into my new life on Earth. She was incredibly wise. She reminded me of the wise elders on Nilrem. She helped me learn about the ocean tides, and how delicate, yet strong the marsh grasses are. When I asked her where all the dragonflies were, she told me it wasn't their time yet. I wasn't sure what she meant, but since my Magic was working just fine, I wasn't concerned. I flew all over the marsh, wondering if Grandpa and my family got their planets confused. Maybe it was some other planet where my Magic wouldn't work. Using my inner powers on this planet was easy, not a big deal. I kept imagining how my family would be proud of me when I told them how great I had been on Earth.

CHAPTER FOUR

MY BEST FRIEND — DARVY

One day, as I was having an enjoyable conversation with some friendly ghost crabs that were scurrying about in the white sand, I saw my first Earth dragonfly.

The funny thing about that moment was that I already felt like I knew him. He didn't remind me of Nilremian elders like Lark did. He reminded me of Merly, even though he didn't look like him. All Nilremian dragonflies, male and female, are rounded. This Earth dragonfly looked skinny to me, though his intricate, green and purple wings were beautiful and perfectly formed. He had a super-friendly expression on his face and a relaxed way of flying around the marsh. His name was Darvy.

I can't imagine what Darvy thought the first time he saw me. I wanted to make a good first impression, and proudly tell him who I was and where I was from, but I got a bit shy. So there I was, silent, wearing my Magic hat, a star shining from my tail, and a whole bunch of hearts and stars on my wings. I was looking anxiously in his direction, but I didn't move toward him. What could he have been thinking? I'm still wondering about that, but he looked curiously in my direction, flew over, and introduced himself. I was so excited! Then, taking a deep breath, I told him who I was and where I came from. His face broke into a great big smile, and he asked me if I wanted to spend some time with him.

And that's how it started. Immediately we became best friends. Over the next six weeks, we did everything together. Even though Earth dragonflies can't fly to other planets, they CAN fly really fast both forwards and backwards, and fly up and down with ease, too. We played dragonfly tag a lot. I decided not to use my faster-than-the-speed-of-light speed, because it really didn't seem fair. We told each other silly jokes. I loved to watch him laugh, because his whole body would spin around as he looked at me upside down!

Darvy brought me to meet other dragonflies and all kinds of seaside creatures. He was a *social* dragonfly, if you know what I mean. Everyone loved Darvy. There were always new friends to meet, and everyone enjoyed being with us. I got the feeling he was very proud to be friends with me. My Nilremian wings got brighter and brighter each day I spent with Darvy. I loved him so much! My magic was working magnificently.

Darvy made me feel special, but I think that's because he felt so special himself. He told me human Earthlings have a deep appreciation for dragonflies. Some bird named a painted bunting had told him that she saw drawings and paintings of dragonflies inside people's homes. She even saw humans wearing pictures of dragonflies on their clothes! Darvy thought that was a great compliment. He was glad that humans liked dragonflies.

I wish I could tell you we spent years together flying all over marshy grasses on your planet. That's not what happened. What I am about to tell you is quite sad, yet what I learned from it is extremely powerful. It helped me to become a stronger dragonfly. So please take a deep breath, and prepare yourself.

One day, as we were racing each other to the end of a sand dune on a sunny beach, Darvy suddenly stopped flying. He hovered in the air for a few seconds, and then fell to the ground. I flew down to him immediately and tried to help him get up. But I couldn't get him to move. I kept asking him what was wrong, but he wouldn't answer. Frantically, I begged him to say something. Softly I heard him whisper, "Love You," and then he stopped breathing.

I was hysterical. I didn't understand what was happening. Nothing like this ever happened to me before. I probably didn't tell you yet that Nilremian dragonflies are immortal. We live forever.

When I lived on Nilrem, sometimes dragonflies would "disappear" for a while. One day they were there, and the next day they would be gone! I was told by the dragonfly elders that they went to other dimensions. I'm still not exactly sure what that means, but it wasn't a big deal. When someone I knew disappeared for a while, I knew that sooner or later, he would come back. No dragonfly ever stopped living. Death doesn't exist on Nilrem.

So when I saw Darvy on the ground, not breathing, I got so scared and upset that I couldn't even think. I started yelling and yelling for help. Lark was near the shore that day, so she was the first one to come to see what was going on

As she swam close to me and saw Darvy's lifeless body on the ground, I could tell by her calm that *she* understood what had happened.

Lark solemnly told me Darvy had died. His dragonfly spirit no longer "occupied" his dragonfly body. She was very sad, but said she felt grateful that I had been such a great friend to him. Then she shared something that really, really, SHOCKED me! She said it was normal for Earth dragonflies to live for a short time, and then die and never come back. That sounded crazy to me!

Darvy, being dead, was bad enough. But to realize that it was **normal** for Earth dragonflies to only live a short time? To have the magnificent gift of wings that let you soar through the air and explore new places, and then not have anything at all? What kind of planet *was* this anyway?

I asked Lark if Darvy knew he would live for a short time. She confidently said she was quite sure that he understood his life cycle, as all Earth animals and insects understand theirs. I thought about that, and then I understood. This was why Darvy lived each day with such joy and enthusiasm. He was such a smart dragonfly-guy.

Oh Darvy, I still miss you so much!

CHAPTER FIVE

DARVY'S FUNERAL

Have you ever watched something that didn't seem real? I felt that way when I watched Darvy's funeral. I had never seen a funeral before, so everything was new and strange.

After Lark arrived, all of Darvy's other friends came. Even though everyone looked quite sad and upset, they all seemed to know what to do. Pearlie, the Pelican, carefully lifted up Darvy's body in her beak, and carried it to a flat place on the sand, where the ocean water would not reach. The other sea creatures gathered around and started digging a hole. Once the hole was deep enough, Pearlie gently picked up Darvy's lifeless body and placed it in the hole.

As I watched all of this, I started to cry. Sobbing is a better word for it. I saw tears on some of the faces of Darvy's friends, yet they had a peacefulness about them that I didn't understand. I didn't feel peaceful at all. I felt devastated and confused.

All of Darvy's friends were now standing around the hole with his lifeless body at the bottom. Each one took a turn to speak. I listened as best I could, though it was hard, because I was so upset.

First, Stevie, the Sea Gull, spoke,

"I am proud to say that I was Darvy's friend. He was the kindest dragonfly I have ever met. I will miss him forever."

Henry, the Heron, spoke next,

"Darvy always made me laugh. I looked forward to being with him whenever I could. He was so much fun. He was a great sport in every game. I will always remember him with joy."

Then Pearlie, the Pelican, said,

"Darvy was one of the best joke tellers I ever met. I loved laughing at his jokes; I will miss that so much. I am grateful for the time we spent together."

And one by one, all of his friends said something wonderful about him. When I think back on it now, it was a beautiful celebration of his life, but when it was happening, celebrating was the last thing I wanted to do.

When it was my turn, I wasn't sure I would be able to talk. I blurted something out like,

"I never knew I would meet someone like Darvy on Earth. He was so special to me, and…."

I couldn't finish my words. I think everyone understood why. Darvy and I really loved each other.

Then, one at a time, each friend dropped some sand in the hole and said goodbye to Darvy, 'till he was all covered up.

Lark said his spirit was still alive in another place that many call "heaven". She said it was a place where Darvy's spirit is forevermore happy and peaceful, somewhere we can't see. I was glad to hear that. Maybe it's the same place the mystical dragonflies of Nilrem sometime visit, but I'm not sure.

After Lark spoke, Pearlie put a large grayish colored stone on top of the hole where Darvy's body was buried and everyone went away looking sad, yet calm. The stone looked like the one he and I used to stand on to watch the tide come in. Later on, I realized that the gray stone was a place to visit, where we could go and talk to him, in our hearts.

As everybody went their own way, I just sat by the stone and tried to figure out what had just happened. It was all VERY confusing to me.

CHAPTER SIX

WHAT GRANDPA WAS TALKING ABOUT

I couldn't fly anymore.

Several days after Darvy's funeral, I noticed my wings looked a bit dull. The beautiful hearts and stars that made up my wings were fading and blending into each other. The colors were all muddied up. I had never seen anyone's wings look like this and it scared me. What was even worse, they **felt** different. At first they were just heavy, really heavy, like I'd been flying for hours in the rain, except it wasn't raining.

A week after Darvy's funeral, they were dragging on the ground. I couldn't lift them up to fly any longer. I couldn't even get them to move the way they were supposed to move. All I could do was walk. That was a terrible time for me.

My wings were
    Way
        Dragged
            Down.

And I had lots of feelings I'd never had before.

Some days I felt angry. I kept thinking, why did Darvy have to die? Why couldn't I save him? IT'S NOT FAIR! I flew all the way to Earth to have this happen?

Some days, I felt so sad that I couldn't even move. I just sat down on the ground and cried. I thought I would never be happy again.

Some days I felt so confused that I didn't want to talk to any Earth creature. Even when some of my other friends came around, I told them to go away. Earth creatures were very annoying to me during those days.

All I really wanted to do was to fly back to Nilrem. I would see all my friends and relatives, and **I would tell Grandpa that he was right. My Magic was gone.** But I couldn't. I couldn't even fly to the other side of the marsh. I was a mess.

After what seemed like a very long time, maybe a few months, Lark came to visit me. I cheered up a bit when she came. I somehow didn't feel annoyed when she started talking to me, and I was able to listen.

She told me in that special kind, soft way of hers, that I was grieving because Darvy had died. I'd never heard that word, **grieving,** before. Lark said I was grieving because I **Loved** Darvy.

Because I *loved* him? No, she was all wrong and I argued with her. How could something that helped me create my wings and fly, cause me so much pain? That made no sense.

22

Lark just stayed by me while I yelled and cried in frustration. Then she said,

"Well, didn't you love him?"

"Of course I loved him!" I cried.

"Tell me about it."

So I did. I told her how I loved Darvy. I loved every moment we spent together, the games we played, the laughter we shared, and the quiet moments we spent alone just staring at the ocean. I cherished those memories, and I always would.

At that moment, I realized she was right. I was feeling grief because I felt so much love for him. I knew I still loved him, even though he was no longer with me.

Then something familiar started to happen. As I was feeling the love I had for Darvy, I felt the outline of the stars and hearts on my wings become more pronounced. The more I talked about Darvy, the clearer the shapes appeared.

Lark left. In the days after her visit, I started to feel better. I still couldn't fly, but I decided to walk around the marsh to see how everyone else was doing.

All of Darvy's friends were doing fine. They were very wise. They always knew that Darvy wasn't going to live long, so they chose to enjoy each moment they had with him.

Even though they missed him, they understood how his life was meant to be lived. They were happy to see me walking stronger, and still wanted to be my friends.

Lark came by to check on me a few days later, and said something to me that I never expected her to say.

"Aren't you a Magical Dragonfly who used your special magic to grow your wings and fly? Aren't you still that same Magical Dragonfly?"

Shocked, I looked Lark straight in her eyes and said, "I AM still a Magical Dragonfly."

"Then BE yourself and create some Magic!" she said, and swam away.

In that instant, I remembered the special rhyme that was told to me when I was a young dragonfly without wings:

The Magic of your wings is this
They grow from what's inside.
>   *Your thoughts and feelings are the key,*
>   *So expand your Love to fly!*
>>   *Focus, little dragonflies*
>>   *Expand your Love to fly,*
>>>   *Focus, little dragonflies*
>>>   *Expand your Love to fly!*

That was it! My thoughts and feelings from all the grieving had really made me dragged-down. But now I knew that I didn't have to stay that way. I could still use my inner powers. I could still think Loving thoughts about everything in my life, including Darvy, who was still in my heart. I could still feel Love for him and everyone else. I didn't have to see Darvy to know that I still loved him.

I felt a shift inside me. Something felt more powerful than ever before. A deep, intense surge of loving energy moved through me. I felt connected to everything and everyone here on Earth.

It was okay that death was part of this planet. That didn't have to stop me from anything. My wings felt stronger than ever, and the colors were, too! I felt like I could fly faster than any other Dragonfly in the Universe! I was proud to be a Magical, Mystical Dragonfly!

And now I understood why Grandpa didn't tell me about death on planet Earth. I might have gotten scared and decided not to go. He wanted me to face this great challenge on my own. He knew how magnificent I would feel if I could use my Magic in the face of something so devastating. And I did! Wow, was Grandpa smart. I was so grateful to him. I guess I grew up a bit that day.

I joyfully flew around the marsh, visiting all my friends. I announced that I was feeling great because I was using my Magic again. They were **so** happy to see me flying because they knew I was moving through all the grief I felt from Darvy's death.

CHAPTER SEVEN

IT'S TIME TO GO HOME !

It was time to end my Earth adventure and fly home. I was anxious to tell Grandpa what happened, so he could be proud of me. I said my loving good-byes to my Earth friends, and thanked them for making me feel so much at home on this different planet.

The last friend I chose to say good-bye to was Lark. She'd supported me every step of the way. I figured she'd be happy about my flying back home, so I was surprised when she wasn't. She wanted me to stay.

That's when things got interesting again. Lark told me something that I will never, ever forget.

Lark said, "Mystie, there's something you need to know about this planet. It's really challenging for Earth children to lose someone they love.

Even though they might understand that no one, not even a pet lives forever, it's not easy for them. It would be great if they could learn how to move through their grief the same way that you did."

"That's silly," I replied. "How could Earth children magically grow wings?"

Jumping out of the water and making her perfectly pitched dolphin-sound, Lark laughed.

"It's not about helping them grow wings, Mystie. It's about reminding them that they, too, can use their inner powers to move through grief. Their "wings" come from their spirit!"

She told me to take a few days and think about what she had said. After all, she reminded me, since I was a wise, Mystical, Magical Dragonfly, I would *know* what decision to make!

I took a week to think and feel about what she said. As I did, my wings began to glow more and more. The yellow star on my tail was shining as bright as I ever saw it. I took a dozen trips around your entire planet with lightning speed.

Finally, I went to see Lark to tell her that I had decided to stay. Naturally, she was delighted to hear that! Then I asked her how I was supposed to know what children to visit.

"I know," was all that she said.

"You know?" I asked. "What do you know?"

She said dolphins are special mammals who know much about what's happening on Earth. She said she could tell which children needed visiting and that my skills would work quite well. She said if I stayed long enough, I could choose to share my wisdom and compassion with lots of children.

"Now to get started," she said, "Your first visit is to a young girl named Christina. Her beloved pet dog, Emrys, is going to die and Christina will have a tough time getting through her grief. Go and help her, Mystie."

Off I went, beginning my New Adventure-

For the Love of All Earthlings,

one child at a time!

Someday I WILL fly back to Nilrem and tell my family everything that happened. I miss them, but I figure there are lots and lots of children who will become my new friends. You, along with all my marsh friends, can be my new Earth family. Maybe together, we can create another Magical Planet of Love like Nilrem.

THE BEGINNING

I DID visit Christina, just liked Lark asked. She was grieving about the death of her precious dog, Emrys. She felt better after we met. I love making new friends with Earth children. If you want to know how Christina moved through her grief, check out For the Love of Emrys.

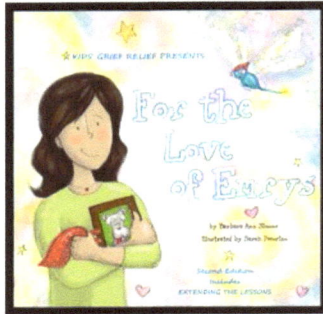

I also made another friend named Jake. His grief caused him to be very angry. If you want to know how Jake moved through his anger and grief, check out For the Love of Mr. Max.

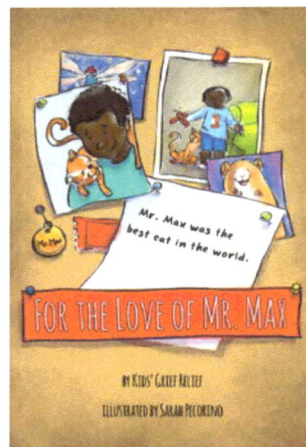

Hi, I'm Mystie. What's Dragon - You - Down ?

KIDS' GRIEF RELIEF

Grief Support to Empower Bereaved Children

Reflections from
Diary of a Mystical Dragonfly !
(a.k.a For the Love of Darvy)

The following exercises are questions for you to reflect upon during the grieving process. As you take the time to clear your heart and mind about what you are going through, you give yourself the opportunity to access your own inner power to help you move through the loss of your loved one – no matter it be a person or a pet.

There are no right or wrong answers, as the journey through grief is your own personal experience. Yet, the way through grief is based upon some universal ideas.

They are:
1. Your thoughts and feelings create your experience.
2. You can choose your thoughts and feelings.
3. You have control over your own thoughts and feelings.
4. Through choosing LOVE, which is a powerful energy inside you, you create a joyful and fulfilled life, even as you experience grief.

You can do these exercises by yourself, or choose a family member or friend to share them with. You can also do them in a group setting.

These exercises correspond to each chapter from the story *Diary of a Mystical Dragonfly* ! You can do as many as you feel comfortable with at any time. You can also revisit the questions again and again, noticing how your answers change as you move through your grief.

There is room for you to write, or you may just want to think about the answers – it's up to you !

CHAPTER ONE
I AM A MAGIAL DRAGONFLY

1. What do you put after your "I Am" statement? Make a list of inner qualities that describe you. For example, I am brave or I am kind.

I Am
I Am
I Am
I Am
I Am

Has your I Am changed at all since the loss of your special someone?
Notice that.

Are you satisfied with your I Am statements? Are there any you would change?
Notice that.

2. How aware are you of your Inner Spirit? - The part inside you that knows who you are (beyond what you look like) and knows what's best for you? On a scale of one to ten, ten being VERY AWARE, how would you rate yourself?

3. List some times in your life when you felt your Inner Spirit.

4. Think about some times when you know you didn't listen to your Inner Spirit.Did you learn something about yourself?

" Getting in touch with your Inner Spirit
will help you move through your grief ! "

CHAPTER TWO
MYSTIE GROWS HER WINGS

1. No matter what age you are, you have already had major accomplishments. What are they?

2. What were the hardest ones/ the easiest ones?

3. What are some of the accomplishments your loved one achieved?

4. Mystie grew her wings using the power of Loving thoughts and feelings. List some loving thoughts and feelings you have for yourself and others. For example, "I like being who I am." "I feel good about my life. " "My friends are really fun to be with".

5. How easy is it to have positive thoughts and feelings for yourself? Notice that.

6. Have your thoughts and feelings about yourself changed since the death of your loved one ?   Notice that.

7. Are there some thoughts and feelings you would like to get rid of?

" Thinking positive thoughts, and feeling positive emotions,

are Magic keys to living a fun life ! "

CHAPTER THREE
MYSTIE FLIES to EARTH

1. How do you usually react/ respond to new experiences in your life? Are you someone who likes to try new things, or are you more content with what you are familiar with. Notice that.

2. Mystie was determined to fly to Earth even though grandpa was not too happy with her choice. How would YOU have handled grandpa?

3. Mystie and Lark, the dolphin, made friends. What qualities do you have that make YOU a good friend?

4. What qualities do your friends have that you really enjoy?

5. Have your friendships changed since the death of your loved one ?

6. Do you have the same friends that you had a few years ago?

7. Do you think you will have the same friends in a few years from now?

" Being a good friend really attracts
good friends to you ! "

CHAPTER FOUR
MY BEST FRIEND DARVY

1. Think about: What were some of the favorite times you spent with your loved one ?

2. What were some of the feelings you had when you shared time with your loved one ?

3. How do you think your loved one felt about you? How does that make you feel ?

4. What is your favorite memory of your loved one ?

5. Are there some qualities of your loved one that you would like to also demonstrate? For example, perhaps your loved one was a really good cook, or perhaps really great at fixing up houses. If it was a pet, perhaps your loved one was a good listener, or a loyal friend.

6. What special things do you have that remind you of your loved one ?

7. Write a poem, create a song, draw or paint a picture that will always remind you of your relationship to your loved one.

" It's important for you to have something or
someplace special to remind you of your loved one.

Whenever I really miss Darvy,
I fly over to the place where he is buried and sit quietly,
thinking about some of the things we used to do. "

CHAPTER FIVE
SAYING GOODBYE

You have the right to know how your loved one died. Are you satisfied with what you know about how he or she died? If not, what else would you like to know? Who can you ask to find the answers?

1. If you experienced the funeral:

    a. What was the worst part? The easiest part?

    b. How did your family members respond to the funeral? What were the different ways they responded?

    c. How did your friends respond?

2. If your loved one was cremated: How do you feel about that?

3. The feeling of loss is tremendously magnified during the death of someone we love. What other losses have you experienced in your life? For example, perhaps you moved away and lost a good friend or you miss a place you used to go to all the time. How did you handle those losses?

4. How are your beliefs about where your loved one is now helping you through your loss?

" I really believe that I will someday see Darvy again! "

CHAPTER 6
WHAT GRANDPA WAS TALKING ABOUT

Mystie couldn't fly after the death of her beloved Darvy, the Earth dragonfly. Are there things you feel like you can't do right now because you lost your loved one?

1. Do you think that will change?

2. Mystie's thoughts and feelings were "dragon-her-down". When you feel "dragged down", what are you thinking/ and or feeling?

3. It's normal and natural to have a lot of different feelings when someone you loved has died. Here's a list of some of them - notice the ones you feel:

a. Mad
b. Sad
c. Upset
d. Confused
e. Worried
f. Angry
g. Betrayed
h. Lonely
i. Lazy

4. How would you like to feel?

" It's normal to miss a loved one,

whether it is a person or a pet.

It's okay.

What's not okay

is to stay "dragged down". "

CHAPTER 7
IT'S TIME TO GO HOME

As Mystie moved through the grieving process, she became aware of the thoughts and feelings that were "dragging her down".

Because of her awareness, she was able to **change** her thoughts and feelings, and fly again. She accepted Darvy's death, realizing that she would always love him, no matter what.

Ultimately, she made the decision to move on with her life, and to love again.

MYSTIE CHOSE LOVE !

" Are YOU ready ?

If not, it's okay.

You WILL be ready when you choose to be.

You WILL be ready when you choose LOVE ! "

KIDS' GRIEF RELIEF

Hi, I'm Mystie.
What's
Dragon - You - Down ?

www.KidsGriefRelief.org

A 501(c)(3) NonProfit

Grief Support to Empower Bereaved Children

For free downloads of special activities,

and additional items to empower bereaved children,

go to:

www.KidsGriefRelief.org/Products.html

We appreciate your donations to Kids' Grief Relief !

Your generosity allows us to gift materials
to bereaved children worldwide,
through schools and hospices.

visit :

www.KidsGriefRelief.org/Donate.html

www.KidsGriefRelief.org

STORYBOOKS   AGE-SPECIFIC PACKAGES   ACCESSORIES

Where Compassion Meets Wisdom

Free Downloads   A 501 (c)(3) Non-Profit   Insightful Blogs

49